Caring Newcastle: The History of Newcastle's Hospitals and Medical School

Ken Smith & Dr Tom Yellowley

ISBN: 9780993195662

Published by:
City of Newcastle Upon Tyne
Newcastle Libraries
Tyne Bridge Publishing, 2017
www.tynebridgepublishing.org.uk

Modern images by Dr Tom Yellowley.

Other images courtesy of Newcastle Libraries, Newcastle University Medical School, the RVI Archives, Robinson Library and Walton Library.

Acknowledgements:

The authors and publisher wish to extend their grateful thanks to Newcastle University for its generous sponsorship of this book.

The authors would also like to thank the following for their kind help: Prof. Julia Newton, Prof. Andrew Fisher, Ian Johnson, Gillian Johnston, Lawrence Rangecroft and David Scott.

Contents

This page: Wounded and recovering servicemen and staff at the Hatton Gallery, Newcastle during its use as part of a military hospital during the First World War

Title page: The Holy Jesus Hospital

Front cover image: Emeritus Professor Fred Page foreground next to trolley, operating at the RVI in 1911 as the guest of Professor Rutherford Morison

Top: The Hospital of St Mary the Virgin pictured in the 18th century. It had become the home of the Royal Grammar School.
Above: What was left of the Hospital of St Mary Magdalene in 1826. It had cared for people suffering from leprosy in Medieval times.

Charity and prayer

Until the foundation of the National Health Service in 1948 the care of the sick and injured poor was reliant on charity or, with the advent of the Poor Law, on relief from parish funds. Charity took the form of subscriptions, gifts and bequests or, in medieval times, the active help given by members of religious orders.

Indeed, the earliest hospitals were run by members of these holy orders, such as priests, monks, friars or nuns, who provided care and accommodation for the poor, sick, infirm and in many cases offered bed and board to pilgrims and travellers. Each hospital tended to specialise in one or perhaps two of these functions.

Among the earliest known hospitals in Newcastle was St Mary Magdalene, near Barras Bridge. Founded during the reign of Henry I (1100-1135), it catered for people suffering from leprosy. Their carers were a 'master, brethren and three sisters'.

A medieval health problem, leprosy is believed by some to have been brought back to England by Crusaders returning from the Holy Land. However, there is no conclusive proof that this was the case and doubt has been cast on the theory.

In addition to those suffering from leprosy, people with various types of skin ailments are thought to have been admitted to the leper, or 'Lazar', hospitals.

Fear of leprosy led to the St Mary Magdalene Hospital being erected on the edge of Newcastle and when the Town Walls were built in the late 13th and 14th centuries the institution was left outside this defensive barrier.

The hospital site was in the area of St Thomas's Church and St Mary's Place. Those who died from leprosy are believed to have been buried near the bridge spanning the Pandon Burn, which ran past the hospital. It is thought that the name for the crossing, Barras Bridge, is derived from the word "barrows", an alternative word for graves. This cemetery, belonging to the hospital, was known as the Maudlin Barrows and the patients were buried there.

By the time of the reign of Henry VIII, leprosy was a rarity in England and those in poverty who were sick were admitted to the St Mary Magdalene Hospital "in times of pestilence" - a reference to the visitations of the bubonic plague.

Another hospital, with an attached chapel, St James's, was set up on the other side of the bridge approximately at the location of today's Great North Museum and this was a sister institution to St Mary Magdalene. It is also believed to have cared for those afflicted with leprosy and perhaps other skin conditions.

There is some evidence that the Maudlin Barrows cemetery may have been close to St James's Hospital and Chapel. The chapel and hospital were eventually demolished and a large house known as St James's Place built on its site. Human bones were discovered during the sinking of two wells behind St James's Place, lending weight to the theory that this was the location of the Maudlin Barrows.

Edward I granted two extra plots of land to the St Mary Magdalene Hospital at the northern end of the Castle Leazes. This area became known as Spital

Tongues. The word 'spital' derives from 'hospital' and 'tongues' are additional strips or portions of land.

Hospitals accommodating the elderly, poor, destitute or pilgrims requiring food and lodging were also to be found in Newcastle.

An institution that almost certainly catered for pilgrims was the Hospital of the Virgin Mary at Jesmond, which was attached to St Mary's Chapel, the ruins of which are still in existence, close to Reid Park Road and Jesmond Dene Road. Pilgrims came from all over Britain to visit the chapel, the Shrine of Our Lady.

Miracles were said to have occurred in the area and were linked to a spring known as St Mary's Well. However, little is known about the hospital or chapel, but they were in existence by 1351.

Other hospitals catered for the poor or elderly. For example, in 1412 wealthy merchant Roger Thornton, who was nine times mayor of Newcastle, founded the Maison de Dieu ("House of God"), to accommodate "nine poor men and four poor women". It was situated next to the town's Quayside in the Sandhill area and part of it occupied land at the eastern end of the present day Guildhall.

Dedicated to St Katherine, the institution was also known as Thornton's or St Katherine's hospital. A priest was appointed warden and he and the residents were instructed to say daily prayers for the soul of Roger Thornton and the townspeople.

Another early charitable institution in Newcastle was the Hospital of St Mary the Virgin, which occupied a site at the junction of today's Neville Street and Westgate Road, in the area of the statue of George Stephenson, close to where the Royal Station Hotel now stands.

Founded by friars during the reign of Henry II (1154-1189), St Mary's provided accommodation for the poor and its hospitality also extended to pilgrims. Much of the site, which included a chapel, was taken over by Newcastle's Royal Grammar School in the reign of Queen Elizabeth I.

The 17th and 18th centuries witnessed the setting up of similar charitable institutions, but not by religious orders. In 1681, Newcastle Corporation founded the Holy Jesus Hospital in the Manors area of the town. This was an almshouse for poor Newcastle Freemen and Freemen's widows or their sons and daughters, provided they were unmarried. The Holy Jesus Hospital buildings survive today in City Road, not far from the Swan House roundabout.

Also still standing in City Road is the Keelmen's Hospital, which opened in 1701. Keelmen operated the oval-

Holy Jesus Hospital in 1935.

Right: The Holy Jesus Hospital.
Below right: The Keelmen's Hospital.

shaped, flat-bottomed craft known as keels which for centuries carried the coal from the north east pits down the Tyne to sailing ships waiting in Shields Harbour or in the lower reaches of the river.

In 1697-1699 the crews of these broad-beamed vessels formed a charity to build the hospital for elderly, sick or infirm keelmen or their widows. The working keelmen paid for it themselves, deducting four pence per river journey from their wages.

Featuring a handsome clock tower and sundial, it stands as a monument to the charity these hardy men displayed towards their fellow workers.

Dr John Moore, Bishop of Ely, said of the Keelmen's Hospital that 'he had heard of and seen many hospitals, the works of rich men; but that it was the first that he had ever seen or heard of that had been built by the poor'.

The increased development of industry, including mining in the 18th century, led to numerous accidents and to a pressing need to treat the victims.

The same century therefore witnessed the foundation of one of the most important hospitals in Newcastle's long history, a hospital which was a major step forward for the care of the sick and injured. This was the Newcastle Infirmary, situated at the top of Forth Banks, where today's Centre for Life stands.

The Infirmary lasted for more than 150 years and from the 1870s onwards, witnessed great advances in surgery. It can be regarded as the first Newcastle 'hospital' in the modern sense of the word.

The Infirmary at Forth Banks

The Newcastle Infirmary at Forth Banks, c.1855-60.

The Newcastle Infirmary was set up in 1751 and its foundation was made possible by a subscription fund established as the result of a letter to a local newspaper. The anonymous letter, to the *Newcastle Courant,* was from a mysterious benefactor signing himself or herself 'B.K.'. His or her identity was never revealed. However, it was rumoured to be a young surgeon named Richard Lambert.

Dated December 28, 1750, the letter, referring to the establishment of voluntary-funded hospitals in several other major cities and towns in Britain, stated:

> "At a time when so noble a spirit of charity is stirring among us, when we see hospitals for the relief of the sick poor, which, of all the various kinds of public charity, deservedly claim the first rank, erected in almost all the large towns in this kingdom, that no such thing should be set on foot in this town is, I think, not a little strange and extraordinary.
>
> Certainly, if in any place, London excepted, an establishment of this kind is necessary, it must be so here. For where are there so great numbers of poor employed or their employment more dangerous than in and about this neighbourhood? Are there not in our coal-works and other manufactures, melancholy accidents almost constantly happening?"

The writer's call for a subscription fund to set up the hospital proved to be a resounding success. Supported by the Press, a committee was formed and soon donations were pouring in. Among the most prominent supporters of the scheme was Newcastle Corporation which made a gift of the land at Forth Banks on which the Infirmary would be built and also contributed £100 towards the fund, a very large sum in the 18th Century.

The scheme proceeded with great speed. The enthusiasm of its supporters led to the hospital being opened even before the new building was erected. A house was acquired in Gallowgate and it began to receive patients in May, 1751. Soon afterwards, there was a need to accommodate more patients and this led to the hiring of rooms in neighbouring houses.

It was not long, however, before building work on the Infirmary at Forth Banks was started. The foundation stone was laid on 5 September, 1751, by the Bishop of Durham, the Right Rev Joseph Butler. The Mayor of Newcastle was among those present.

The Ravensworth Wards, the last extention to the old Infirmary, with the ornamental fountain and statues in front, c1900.

On 8 October 1753, the new hospital was opened to receive its first patients. The cost of construction and equipment amounted to £3,697. One of its first surgeons was Richard Lambert, the young man credited with writing the letter that had started the project.

Surgeon George Haliburton Hume, in his *History of the Newcastle Infirmary* (1906), tells us that the hospital building featured a stone ashlar exterior lined with brick. It was grouped around two sides of a quadrangle, with a frontage to the south and east. The south front was three storeys high with a basement and the east front consisted of two storeys.

The first floor of the south-facing wing contained a hall which was used as a board room, and a surgery, a physicians' room, a parlour for the matron and a chapel. The second storey featured three male wards, named the Newcastle, the Durham and the Northumberland. In the attic, or third storey, was an operating theatre and two other wards, the Cheselden and Harvey.

The first storey of the east wing contained two wards for men, one known as the B.K. in salute to the letter writer, and the Job. On the second floor were three wards for women, the Magdalen, the Lazarette and the Butler.

The grounds of the Infirmary included a burial area and a garden with an ornamental fountain surrounded by statues. In the earlier years, the Skinner Burn, a small tributary of the Tyne, could be seen flowing along the western edge of the site. Later, the burn was culverted and topped with infilling to extend the garden.

Initially, ninety beds were provided and in the first year 167 in-patients and 178 out-patients were received. These admissions were by subscriber's letter. This meant that only patients recommended by people who had given money to fund the hospital could receive care and treatment.

The hospital admitted many patients injured in accidents, and surgery was a principal part of its work. In 1774, the governors of the institution decided to exclude fever patients from its wards. A number of other classes of patient were also refused admission.

Newcastle historian Eneas Mackenzie, writing in the 1820s, lists those excluded from the Infirmary as 'women big with child, children under seven years of age, except those upon whom surgical operations are to be performed, persons judged to be incurable, or in a dying condition, or labouring under insanity, the smallpox, or other infectious distemper, or afflicted with cancer not admitting of operation, or with consumption, scrofula, or dropsy, in the last stage.'

Yet there was compassion in evidence. Mackenzie asserts: 'Persons meeting with sudden accidents, or labouring under diseases requiring *immediate* help of surgery, are admitted, without recommendation at any hour of the day or night'. All other patients were admitted by a recommendation letter and only on a Thursday.

Despite the recommendations, it seems the conduct of some patients in the 18th century was not always beyond reproach. Hume declares that 'disorderly, dirty and drunken' habits among patients led to strong reprimands from the House Committee. On some occasions the names of those who misbehaved and their offences were posted up and read out in the wards.

There were occasional complaints from patients about the food and drink. Hume describes an amusing episode in May, 1754, when a complaint about the meat and beer was judged by the committee to be without foundation. The complaining patients were severely reprimanded and ordered to have toast and water for a week.

It was a distinctly unsympathetic reaction, but the committee seems to have taken on board part of the complaint. They ordered that the quantity of malt in the beer should be increased. At this period a small brewery was situated within the hospital grounds. Most water was unsafe to drink.

A number of 'house visitors' were appointed to the hospital to comfort the patients and perhaps also to keep an eye on proceedings. The house visitors were in earlier years expected to attend the funerals of patients, presumably those buried in the cemetery in the hospital grounds.

The medical staff at first consisted of four physicians and two surgeons, but in 1760 two more surgeons were appointed, making numbers equal. Other appointments included a matron and apothecary.

During the second half of the 18th century and early 19th century only a small number of nurses were employed at the Infirmary and their pay was low. Hume suggests that it was likely that much of the time patients were left to nurse each other. Convalescents probably shared with the nurse the task of looking after the more seriously affected patients.

As late as 1865 there were only eleven nurses employed. In 1868, there were thirteen. This was a ratio of one nurse to 13.4 occupied beds.

A significant step forward in the training of nurses came in the late 1860s with the appointment of a nurse superintendent who could provide the necessary education. During the earliest years of the hospital the few nurses that were employed had been untrained and most were probably unable to read or write.

As well as the scarcity of nursing staff, another drawback beset the institution. Throughout much of its life its wards suffered from overcrowding, and an excess of patients only added to the risk of infections spreading.

In an attempt to solve this problem a westwards extension to the building was erected in 1801-1803. However, a continuing increase in the population and therefore an increase in patients meant the problem did not go away.

The new wards were divided into small apartments in the belief that this would combat the spread of infection. It was soon evident that the accommodation provided little relief from the overcrowding. In 1804, a report by the Infirmary's

House Committee told the governors that more beds were "crowded into some of the apartments than they were intended to contain, and several instances have occurred when two patients have been put into one bed".

At this time, the average length of stay for patients in the hospital was fifty-four days, an extremely long period by present-day standards. This contributed greatly to the overcrowding.

A Lister carbolic spray which was made in Newcastle in the 1870s and was almost certainly used at the old Infirmary. (Tom Yellowley, courtesy of the Robinson Library, Newcastle.)

The problem continued and in 1852 work began on a second extension to the hospital. This would add six new wards and provide an additional 144 beds. The extension, at right angles to the rest of the building, was designed by renowned North-East architect John Dobson and completed by the end of 1854.

The official opening took place in January 1855. Presiding at the ceremony, in the aptly named Percy Ward, was Algernon, Fourth Duke of Northumberland, who had contributed £1,000 towards the new building.

Among the surgeons at the hospital during the 19th century was Dr Charles John Gibb, who is mentioned in the Tyneside anthem *The Blaydon Races*.

Gibb was house surgeon from 1849 to 1854 and honorary surgeon from 1855 to 1870. By all accounts he was much appreciated by his patients and on leaving his post as house surgeon he developed a large medical practice in Newcastle and the surrounding area. Dr Gibb was also a much valued lecturer at the Newcastle Medical School.

In 1853 the town was hit by a major outbreak of cholera. This serious disease affected patients in the Infirmary and six died.

The hospital staff won admiration for the way they dealt with the crisis. As the cholera epidemic raged, the Infirmary opened its doors to all, free of charge and gave comfort to worried and anxious people. Some presented themselves at the hospital believing they were suffering from early symptoms of the disease and were offered medicine and advice. The wards of the uncompleted extension, known appropriately as the Dobson Wing, were used to relieve pressure of numbers during the outbreak, which caused 1,533 deaths in the town.

In the following year, 1854, there was a further emergency. Gateshead quayside was hit by a major fire and this resulted in a great explosion which devastated and set fire to buildings on the other side of the Tyne in Newcastle. The tragedy resulted in the deaths of 53 people.

A total of 123 injured victims of the disaster were treated at the Infirmary and sixty of these were admitted as in-patients. The wards of the new wing played an important part in enabling the hospital to cope with this emergency and a new, large accident room, which had opened only two days before the explosion, greatly assisted initial assessment and treatment.

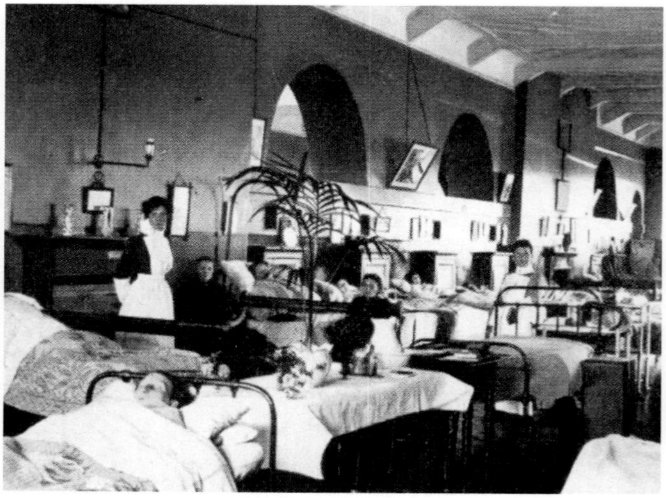

Overcrowded - a female surgical ward at the old Infirmary.

The year 1858 brought yet another crisis. Major outbreaks of sepsis – infection of wounds, often after surgery – struck the wards, old and new. These infections included erysipelas, a serious skin condition.

According to Hume, another sepsis scourge was pyaemia 'which in former days had so often stepped in to mar the success of many a well planned operation'. This condition invaded the wards again. Pyaemia proved fatal before the introduction of antibiotics.

The next three years were also badly affected by sepsis and further outbreaks continued to occur into the 1860s, reaching a high point in 1867.

However, within a decade the situation was to change. In 1874, a new senior house surgeon was appointed, George Beatson, who brought about a vast improvement. He had worked as a house surgeon with Joseph Lister, the pioneer of antiseptic technique, in Edinburgh. Beatson introduced Lister's methods into the hospital and there was an immediate improvement. Carbolic acid sprays during operations and the use of carbolic acid in the washing of hands and surgical instruments became the norm. Carbolic acid was also sprayed on dressings.

A report on the state of the Infirmary for 1875 stated that there had "not been a single case" of sepsis during the year, often referred to as 'hospital disease'. Succeeding years proved that the introduction of the antiseptic (sometimes termed 'aseptic') method was a major breakthrough.

Antiseptic measures and the use of chloroform as an anaesthetic greatly widened the range of operations that could be performed. It also led to an increase in the number of operations. They soared from 297 in 1876 to 908 in 1884, a rise of over 200 per cent.

Yet this trend increased the overcrowding problem. Staff members were keen to see a new hospital built, but after discussions it was decided to build a temporary extension, which became known as the Ravensworth Wards. The building, completed in 1885, provided an extra fifty beds and brought the total number of beds to 270.

Wealthy philanthropist Sir William Armstrong, later Lord Armstrong of Cragside, founder of Newcastle's Elswick Works and Shipyard, contributed £1,000 of the £2,260 needed to construct the extension. Sir William also paid for the provision of a new operating theatre on the ground floor.

In 1887, came another milestone for the Infirmary. The subscription system was abolished and it was made a free hospital. It was found that the subscriptions were failing to cover the cost of caring for and treating the patients. In addition, the poor or those on low incomes had been forced to rely on the charity of subscribers and many failed to gain admission.

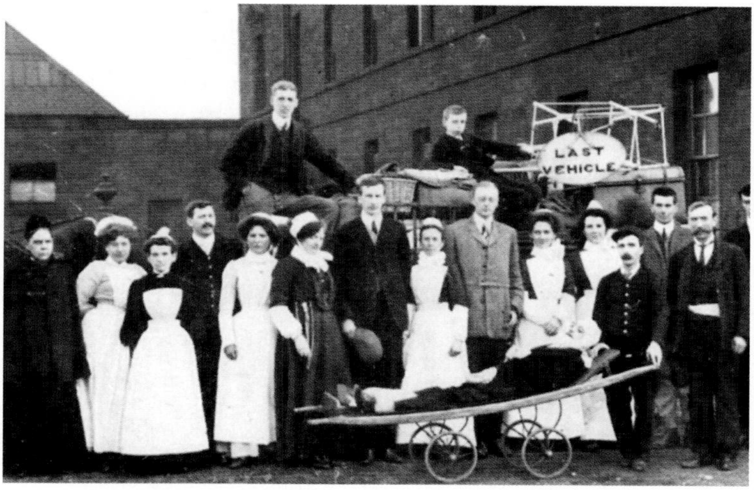

The last patient leaving the old Infirmary in September 1906.

There was, however, a condition attached to this charitable move. The House Committee made it clear that although the hospital was now described as free, it reserved the right to charge patients who were able to pay for the whole or part of their maintenance. The abolition of the subscription letter system led to working people of Newcastle and its surrounding area increasing their support for the hospital. Collections made at their places of employment began pouring in to help fund the Infirmary.

In 1886, the working people of 17 firms in Newcastle, County Durham and Northumberland had contributed £317 to the hospital. After 1887, the figure soared. In 1889, employees of 112 firms contributed £1,552.

Also in the 1880s, nine working men from various firms were elected to the House Committee. In 1905, the number of working men on the committee was increased to 12. Working men also served as governors of the hospital.

In 1887, the same year in which the recommendation letter system was abolished, Queen Victoria's Jubilee was celebrated and the monarch granted the hospital the title Royal. It now became the Royal Infirmary for the Counties of Newcastle upon Tyne, Northumberland and Durham.

Yet despite the progress made in accommodation, over the years the hospital had become surrounded by urban and industrial development. Further expansion was difficult on the restricted site, but lengthy discussions about the possibility of building a new hospital at the same location came to nothing.

The steam railway was to prove another problem. The hospital was close to the lines running into and out of the Central Station. Noise from the engines was a constant nuisance.

Even in Mackenzie's day in the early 19th century smoke from the chimneys of the town and glass factories had proved to be an annoyance. Adding to the limitations of the site was the presence of the adjacent cattle market.

The Infirmary had done much good work over more than 150 years but by the 1890s many believed it was time for major change.

Fevers and home visits

The former Fever Hospital in Bath Lane, which opened in 1804.

The Fever Hospital, also known as the House of Recovery, was opened in 1804 in the Warden's Close, an area immediately outside the western section of the Town Walls.

An earlier plan to open a fever ward at the Infirmary was not implemented because spread of infection was feared. The plan had divided the opinion of physicians and surgeons.

The land for the Fever Hospital in Bath Lane was gifted by Newcastle Corporation and funding for construction raised by subscriptions.

Mackenzie states that great attention was paid to 'purification' of the rooms, bedding and clothing of patients. Writing in the 1820s, he declares that 'since it was first opened in 1804, the progress of fever in this town and the vicinity has been frequently and promptly arrested'.

Patients who could afford to pay were charged two shillings per day and had to provide their own medicines and attendants. The poor could be attended to if their friends or the parish paid the same amount. They were given medicine by an apothecary from the Dispensary who visited the hospital on a daily basis. Wine was among the prescriptions available. Comfort was provided rather than cure.

Diseases suffered by patients included smallpox, cholera and typhoid. As late as 1881, seven patients were reported to have died from smallpox. All had been suffering from the severest form of the illness.

The Fever Hospital closed in 1888 but the building survives today at the northern end of Bath Lane as a reminder of an era when infectious diseases were often rife.

The old hospital, however, was replaced by a new one, the City Hospital for Infectious Diseases in Walkergate in the East End of Newcastle. It opened in the same year that the House of Recovery closed. Patients were admitted with scarlet fever, diptheria and other serious conditions.

In 1948, the NHS was created and it became known as Walkergate Hospital. Eye, ear, nose, throat and respiratory conditions were now treated there. Medical services were also provided for the elderly.

A 'temporary' smallpox hospital was built on the Town Moor in 1882, consisting of single-storey buildings of corrugated iron and wood. It was situated off the southern side of Grandstand Road between the Cow Hill junction and Kenton Road. Today, a track leads from Grandstand Road towards the site of the unit, where there is now a group of trees.

In late 1927, sixty-five men, some of whom were residents of the Newcastle Workhouse and others patients of the Workhouse Hospital in Westgate Road, contracted smallpox. Nearly all were admitted to the Town Moor hospital, but fortunately in this outbreak the illness was mild. Every patient recovered.

A ward at the City Hospital for Infectious Diseases, Walkergate, 1890s.

The hospital could accommodate around 170 patients, although whether this number was ever admitted at any one time is doubtful. The 'temporary' hospital was used as an overflow unit for patients suffering from a variety of infectious diseases and not exclusively for smallpox patients. It was not demolished until around 1957.

A second isolation hospital had been built at Lemington, on the western side of the city. After the advent of the NHS in 1948 it became a unit for geriatric patients.

Another institution that provided care and treatment for the sick and injured was the Dispensary, which opened in 1777 in rooms at the foot of The Side. Dr John Clark, who later became an honorary physician to the Infirmary, was a leading founder of this clinic.

The Dispensary provided medicines, treatment and advice to patients unable to obtain admittance to the Infirmary. According to Mackenzie, they were a 'numerous class of sufferers'. This 'numerous class' were the poor of the town.

Doctors from the Dispensary also carried out home visits to very sick patients and attended those in the Fever Hospital. These were important services for the poor.

After four years at The Side, the Dispensary moved to accommodation off Pilgrim Street, in an alleyway which became known as Dispensary Entry.

In 1790, came another move, this time to a larger home in St John's Lodge, Low Friar Street, close to the Black Friars and behind Newgate Street. The accommodation included two consulting rooms for the physicians and surgeons, lodgings for the apothecary and his assistant, a shop and a waiting room for patients. There was a small laboratory behind the building. The Dispensary does not, however, seem to have ever accommodated in-patients.

The institution was essentially an out-patients' clinic and home visiting service for poor inhabitants of Newcastle and Gateshead. However, a recommendation letter system was in operation. In Mackenzie's day, a subscriber of one guinea could recommend five patients annually.

Prevention was another aspect of this charitable institution's work. Between the spring of 1801 and the autumn of 1826 the staff of the Dispensary vaccinated a total of 20,385 people against smallpox.

In 1839, the Dispensary moved to a new home in Nelson Street. The premises had been specially built to accommodate the institution. This remained its home until 1928 when it moved to New Bridge Street. The letter system was still in operation, but there were also casual patients who turned up for treatment and paid a small fee.

The advent of the National Health Service in 1948 signalled the end for almost all the services offered by the Dispensary as these were now covered by other hospitals, clinics and family doctors in the city, free of charge. Despite this, a free rheumatism and arthritis clinic continued at the New Bridge Street premises on a charitable basis until 1976.

Caring for the 'outcasts'

The Lock Hospital was set up in 1814 to care for women suffering from venereal diseases. Syphilis and gonorrhoea could not be effectively treated before the introduction of antibiotics in the 20th century.

The term 'Lock' is thought to be derived from the rags, also known as 'locks', which were applied to the sores of leprosy patients during the Middle Ages.

The Newcastle Lock Hospital was opened in a rented house near the Pink Tower, in the vicinity of Pink Lane, within the Town Walls. The unfortunate women admitted to this establishment seem to have been mainly prostitutes.

Mackenzie informs us that the doors of the Infirmary were shut against those suffering from venereal diseases and that the affected 'outcast was denied all participation in any of the public benevolent establishments'.

Left: The Dispensary in Nelson Street, 1927.
Above: The earlier Dispensary in Low Friar Street.

The last Newcastle Dispensary, in New Bridge Street.

The Dispensary was the only institution that offered any help 'but its power of extending such relief was necessarily limited to slight cases'.

The opening of the Lock Hospital was first proposed by two 'eminent' surgeons of the town, although Mackenzie does not mention them by name. Many 'gentlemen' are said to have supported the scheme and 'several ladies...sanctioned the undertaking by benefactions'.

Compassion was undoubtedly one motive for the foundation of the hospital, but there was also a view that sheltered accommodation was needed for 'protection of the community'. Mackenzie implies that a suggestion was made to attach secure accommodation to the house 'to discourage the wretched prostitute from relapsing into her former habits'. The idea, however, did not win much support.

When the hospital opened in November 1814 it was 'under the management of a committee of gentlemen'. The Duke of Northumberland and the Bishop of Durham were among those contributing funding.

Around 1824, the Lock Hospital moved to a new home in a street on the west side of the Castle Keep. The institution did not issue annual reports and seems to have kept its affairs largely secret. Mackenzie bemoans this lack of transparency.

A decline in funding led to closure of the hospital around 1829-1830 and its patients were transferred to a ward, known as the Magdalen, at the Infirmary. A third storey had been added to the east wing of the building to open this ward. Many of these patients would undoubtedly have been suffering from syphilis, a serious and widespread health problem before the discovery and introduction of penicillin in the 20th century.

A second dispensary

A dispensary was founded in Gateshead in November 1832 and operated on similar lines to Newcastle's, providing a home visiting service for the poor during sickness and offering advice and treatment to outpatients.

The Gateshead Dispensary was set up as the result of a cholera outbreak that started in late 1831 and raged throughout most of 1832. The epidemic led to the appalling total of 234 deaths, which mainly affected the poorest inhabitants of the town living in insanitary tenements and lodging houses.

Indeed, Gateshead was periodically hit by infectious diseases throughout much of the 19th century and the problem led to the opening of an isolation hospital with thirty-eight beds at Sheriff Hill on Gateshead Fell. This unit was extended in 1904, bringing the bed total to sixty-four.

Yet it became increasingly clear that the town was in need of its own general hospital in addition to the isolation unit. This came in the 1940s when the Queen Elizabeth Hospital was completed on land close to the Sheriff Hill Isolation Hospital.

Generally referred to as the 'QE', the new hospital was officially opened in 1948, although patients began to be admitted in 1944-45. Today, after undergoing many changes, it still serves Gateshead and its surrounding area as a major component of health service provision. An extension to the isolation hospital was completed in 1940 and this was later incorporated into the 'QE'.

The town's Dispensary, which from 1855 to 1946 occupied premises in Nelson Street, on a corner with West Street, carried out much good work, lasting well into the 20th century. Its doctors and nurses made many thousands of home visits to the poor or those on low incomes.

However, the Dispensary ceased to exist in 1948 as the services it provided were now covered by the newly-founded NHS.

The Royal Victoria Infirmary

In 1896, the Mayor of Newcastle, Riley Lord, proposed that a new hospital be built to replace the old Infirmary. His idea was that the hospital would be a fitting tribute to Queen Victoria, whose Diamond Jubilee was to be celebrated the following year.

At a public meeting in October 1896 subscriptions amounting to over £38,000 were pledged towards the scheme. The money kept on flooding in. By Diamond Jubilee Day, June 22, 1897, the figure had reached more than £100,000.

In addition, wealthy benefactor John Hall gifted a further £100,000, with the proviso that the new hospital be built on a site near the Town Moor.

Afterwards, came another major contribution. William Watson-Armstrong, heir and great nephew of Lord Armstrong of Cragside, gave another £100,000. The fund was now boosted to £300,000. Of this total, £20,000 had been contributed by "working men of the district".

Further help came from another direction. Newcastle City Council and the

No. 109

Z

ROYAL PAVILION.

This Ticket is for one person only.

The only Road is by way of St. Thomas Street from Percy Street.

The Royal Victoria Infirmary.

Queen Victoria Road, Newcastle-upon-Tyne.

Opening Ceremony by His Majesty The King,

July 11th, 1906.

ADMIT Holder to ROYAL PAVILION.

Entrance by Gate opposite Armstrong College.

The Holder must be in the Pavilion not later than 11.15 o'clock, and remain seated until the Royal Party leave.

W. Sutton Jr.

Secretary of Reception Committee.

This Ticket must be produced at the Entrances to the New Infirmary and the Royal Pavilion, and to any Police Officer on the Route.

Above: A ticket for the opening of the RVI by Edward VII in 1906.
Right: The statue of the young Queen Victoria is unveiled on the opening day.
Below: A celebratory mood in Queen Victoria Road for the opening of the RVI.

Freemen of Newcastle gave ten acres of land on the Castle Leazes as the site for the new infirmary. The scheme was now firmly on course for success.

The Prince of Wales, later Edward VII, laid the foundation stone on June 20, 1900, and in the same year Queen Victoria commanded that the name of the hospital should be the Royal Victoria Infirmary.

Five years afterwards, the magnificent new hospital, one of the largest in Britain, was officially opened by Edward VII, accompanied by his wife, Queen Alexandra, on July 11, 1906. Two of the RVI wards were named the Edward and the Alexandra.

During the opening ceremony, King Edward declared that it was a 'satisfaction for us to know that the workers have given so generously towards the fund'. He

also announced: ‘I am of the opinion that the chief magistrate of this city should bear the title Lord Mayor, and I will have much pleasure in giving the necessary instructions to grant it.’

On the same day, Edward unveiled a statue of his mother, Queen Victoria, outside the main entrance. The white marble figure of Victoria as a young woman at about the time of her coronation is by George Frampton, RA, and was provided by Riley Lord, who, as we have seen, led the move to have the hospital built. He was knighted for his efforts.

Benefactor William Watson-Armstrong was later created the second Lord Armstrong, an acknowledgement of his contribution to building and supporting the hospital. He served as chairman of the House Committee.

On September 17, 1906, the first patients were transferred from the old infirmary to the new.

In 1907, its first full year of operation, the Royal Victoria Infirmary (RVI), treated more than 6,000 in-patients and over 93,000 out-patients. In 1913, the figures had risen to over 8,500 in-patients and more than 101,700 out-patients. It is of interest to note that by 1928, nearly half of all patients were from County Durham.

The RVI has always been a regional hospital and from its earliest days a major teaching hospital, working in close association with Newcastle’s medical school. In so doing, it has continued the tradition of teaching started at the old Infirmary.

As originally built, the RVI contained twenty wards spread over two floors, five operating theatres, an accident room, an out-patients’ department, a nurses’ home and a Byzantine-style chapel dedicated to St Luke (the chapel in the old Infirmary had also been dedicated to the saint). Surgical wards were on the ground floor and medical and gynaecological wards on the upper. The total number of available beds was 425.

The out-patients’ department was situated on the lower ground floor and featured a large patients’ waiting hall, a dispensary and its own operating theatre.

The ground floor was centred on a long, east-west corridor, with wings, known as pavilions, containing the wards branching off to the north and south.

Each pavilion had its own verandah and coal fires for heating were placed in the centre of every ward with smoke ducts that ran beneath the floor and then upwards to a chimney.

The east-west corridor and pavilion arrangements were duplicated on the upper floor. At the eastern end of the corridors were the children’s wards.

The walls of the wards were of coated cement, making them non-absorbant and the lower sections featured tiled dados. All corners were rounded to allow for easy cleaning and to combat dust.

The administrative offices, including the board room and main entrance foyer, were positioned off the central area of the corridor, facing south. This block became known as Peacock Hall after the birds and feathers which were depicted on its leather wallpaper. The tall clock from the old Infirmary was installed on a landing of the stairway, where it remains to this day.

The Nurses’ Home, capable of accommodating around 100, was built to the west of the main building. The home and main building were connected to each

kwise from top left: 1) The RVI in its early years. 2) The statue of Queen Victoria in front of the administration block the RVI. 3) Patients in the Outpatients' Waiting Hall before the First World War. 4) The Peacock Hall Administration block today. 5) Ward 4 at the RVI c.1925.

other by a conservatory linked to the ground floor east-west corridor. A westward extension of the Nurses' Home was completed in 1932.

In 1918, the last year of the First World War, a second unit, known as the Ministry of Pensions Hospital, was opened to the north of the main building. This hospital, featuring three pavilion blocks and wooden huts, was designed to help the RVI cope with the large number of war casualties needing treatment and rehabilitation. Two temporary extra wards were constructed on the main hospital site as another wartime contingency measure.

At the start of the conflict 200 beds were reserved for the treatment of servicemen and the out-patients' hall was converted into a forty-two bed ward.

Also during the war, the nearby Armstrong College and Hatton Gallery buildings, now part of Newcastle University, were taken over to become the First Northern General Hospital, Territorial Force, for the treatment of wounded and disabled soldiers.

The extra demands resulting from the war meant that the doctors, surgeons and nurses of the RVI were under great pressure. A large number of medical and nursing staff had joined the armed forces.

Retired members of staff returned to the RVI to fill the gaps left by this exodus. Medical students in the last two years of their training also made an important contribution to staffing the hospital during this period.

A few years after the end of the war, the Ministry of Pensions Hospital buildings were absorbed into the RVI and became known as the Leazes Wing or Leazes Hospital.

Discussions had taken place about the need for a convalescent home to relieve overcrowding at the RVI, but lack of money to provide such an institution had not been forthcoming.

This impasse was eventually removed when Lieut. Colonel C.H. Innes Hopkins gifted to the hospital a mansion in Ryton, known as Ryton Towers, as a memorial to his two sons who had lost their lives during the war. The property was officially opened as a convalescent home in 1923.

Ryton Towers was used by recovering patients until 1934 when it was replaced by Castle Hill convalescent home at Wylam. This was the gift of Geoffrey Stirling Newall, as a memorial to his mother and father. This generous benefactor also paid for modifications to the Castle Hill property to make it more suitable to accommodate patients. The home at Wylam was surrounded by fifteen acres of parkland and had an ornamental garden complete with topiary.

Castle Hill convalescent home and the earlier property at Ryton undoubtedly helped to reduce the average length of stay in the RVI from nineteen days in 1907 to 11.42 days in 1947. In addition, help also came with the provision in 1936 of the Greycourt convalescent home for children, not far from Riding Mill. It was the gift of Norman Newall, chairman of the hospital finance committee. However, a disastrous fire put the building out of service in 1940.

A major addition to the hospital came in 1933 when a new orthopaedic block was opened between the Leazes Wing and the main RVI building. Its facilities included two wards, a fracture clinic and an operating theatre.

Many other extensions and buildings were erected over the next 40 years on the RVI site as medical facilities expanded to meet the needs of modernisation and

The new RVI, with the Great North Children's Hospital on the left.

growing demand. Demolition of some of the older buildings on the site also took place, including the old Leazes Wing.

The number of beds increased from 420 in 1907 to 600 in 1947. During the same period in-patient numbers rose from 6,445 to 19,333. Operations increased from 5,678 to 18,026.

In 1992, came a milestone when a major extension to the hospital was opened, the new Leazes Wing. It includes, among other facilities, the Newcastle maternity unit and gynaecology wards. This wing is at the western end of the site.

The year 1996 witnessed the opening of a further new building, the Claremont Wing, where ophthalmic services are based.

In 2005, work started to continue the transformation of the RVI into a modern, state-of-the-art hospital fit for the 21st century. An impressive new building, known as the New Victoria Wing, was opened in 2010, featuring a very large atrium leading to many facilities, including various out-patients' departments, women's services, critical care services and an infectious diseases unit. A helicopter pad is located on top of the wing so that patients can be flown in for urgent treatment.

New facilities also include the round-shaped, green-coloured Great North Children's Hospital, where a wide range of advanced medical services for the treatment of sick children are based, and a superb accident and emergency department, stated to be one of the best equipped in the UK, which includes a trauma centre, a minor injuries unit and a children's emergency department.

Most of the old RVI buildings have now been demolished, but Peacock Hall and St Luke's Chapel are among the few that have been retained, standing as eloquent testimony to the humanitarian spirit that led to the foundation of this great regional hospital.

The nursery rhyme tiles

Two of the nursery rhyme tiled pictures.

The RVI's original children's wards were decorated with a wonderful collection of tiled panels depicting characters from nursery rhymes.

The colourful hand-painted tiles were manufactured by the Royal Doulton Company of London and possess great charm. Many of these panels are signed by the artists.

A number of other tiles depict landscapes rather than nursery rhymes.

Both types were carefully preserved when the old buildings were largely demolished and today they grace various areas of the new buildings, including the Great North Children's Hospital and a corridor leading to the Leazes Wing.

This corridor also features the Leazes Bedspread, which was embroidered with flowers by First World War servicemen recovering from their wounds in the old Leazes Hospital (Ministry of Pensions Hospital).

From Rosemary Lane to Leazes Wing

In the autumn of 1760, a lying-in hospital for expectant, poor married women was established at a house in Rosemary Lane, Newcastle, alongside St John's Churchyard.

This maternity hospital, the first to be set up in the town, was – like the old Infirmary - the result of a public subscription fund. A physician, two surgeons, a male midwife and a matron, Mrs Sarah Hudson, were appointed to run the establishment.

From October 1760 to September 1825, a total of 3,193 women gave birth in the Rosemary Lane hospital and twenty-two died. However, at this period the majority of deliveries were conducted in patients' homes. A home birth service for Newcastle had been set up in 1761 by a charity formed for the purpose. This was operated by midwives, with back-up from surgeons and doctors.

In 1819, Thomas Elliott, a surgeon to the Rosemary Lane hospital, began a subscription fund to provide a purpose-built lying-in hospital for poor married women. This would be a replacement for the house in Rosemary Lane. Newcastle Corporation supported the scheme by granting the subscribers a site fronting on to New Bridge Street.

The new maternity hospital, designed by John Dobson, opened in October 1826. Twelve patients could be accommodated in what was described by Mackenzie as a 'remarkably chaste, plain, and substantial stone building in the style of English architecture that prevailed about the end of the reign of Henry VIII'.

The upper floor contained two 'large, light, airy' wards each holding four beds and two smaller wards each accommodating two beds.

Subscribers to the hospital could recommend by letter one patient per year for each guinea they contributed annually.

The rules of the institution were evidently strict. Every woman who wished to be admitted was required to produce a certificate of marriage. No woman could be admitted suffering from a contagious infection, or without a fixed residence, unless her husband was a soldier or sailor. Every patient was also required to bring a child's dress with her.

Mackenzie states: 'Three skilful surgeons attend the hospital in rotation, each of whom are, if need be, to hold consultation with the other surgeons and with the physician. The matron is to deliver in all natural and easy cases'.

The Newcastle Lying-in Hospital at New Bridge Street was to remain in operation for nearly 100 years. In 1858, the home birth charity merged with the hospital, thus bringing domiciliary and hospital services under one organisation. In 1902, an extension to the New Bridge Street building was opened, increasing the number of beds.

The new ward was named in memory of Thomas Cargill Nesham, who had served as surgeon to the institution and as a lecturer in midwifery at the medical school.

Despite this expansion, by 1920 the hospital was proving inadequate to meet increasing demand. In 1923, it was moved to new premises in the former Ragged and Industrial School in Jubilee Road, near City Road and the Keelmen's Hospital. This development was led by pioneering obstetrician and gynaecologist Professor Robert Patten Ranken Lyle. He had arrived in Newcastle from Ireland to take up a post at the medical school in 1899 and later opened a free clinic for women in a house in St Thomas Street. It was not long before he was appointed the first specialist in gynaecology at the RVI.

The former Lying-in Hospital in New Bridge Street.

Major building work to modify the school in Jubilee Road for its new role as a maternity hospital and ante-natal clinic was carried out in 1922-24. The New Bridge Street lying-in hospital building was taken over by the BBC.

The Jubilee Road unit, which had ninety beds, was officially opened on November 24, 1923, by Princess Mary, Viscountess Lascelles, and was appropriately named the Princess Mary Maternity Hospital.

From 1935, the hospital pioneered the use of an emergency service for women undergoing a home birth. If a serious problem arose a 'Flying Squad' would be sent from the Princess Mary to a woman's home to give vital on-the-spot treatment before transfer to hospital. It was the first such service in England and was taken up throughout the country.

The outbreak of the Second World War in 1939 brought a major change for the Princess Mary. It was felt that the location of the unit made it vulnerable to air raids and the decision was taken to move the hospital to a safer site in the city.

One side of the former Princess Mary Hospital near the Great North Road. It was originally an orphanage.

Accordingly, the now empty girls' section of the Northern Counties Orphanage at Moor Edge, near the Great North Road, was taken over for the in-patients of the hospital. The ante-natal clinic and district staff remained at the Jubilee Road building.

The Princess Mary now had a new home, and in 1943 this expanded when the boys' side of the orphanage was taken over to relieve overcrowding. All children had been evacuated from the orphanage in 1939.

In early 1944 an extension was opened which increased the number of beds to ninety-six and in 1949 the hospital underwent extensive reconstruction. Princess Mary, now the Princess Royal, returned in early 1950 to open the improved hospital. Further work to improve facilities was carried out in 1967-1968 and in 1981-1984.

The Princess Mary was not, however, the only maternity unit in Newcastle. Another was operated at the Newcastle General Hospital in Westgate Road for around eighty years. The first maternity department opened there in 1903 with twelve beds and two labour wards.

The number of women delivered increased rapidly during the 1930s. A new maternity department was needed and this was opened in 1939 at the northern end of the General site. In 1947 an ante-natal clinic began operating from a separate building at the hospital.

An extension to the General's maternity department was opened in 1968, which included the provision of two extra wards and two delivery rooms. During the early 1970s births at the unit soared and exceeded those at the Princess Mary.

The 1990s, however, witnessed one of the most significant changes in the history of childbirth provision in the city. This came when the Newcastle General Hospital maternity department and the Princess Mary Maternity Hospital were amalgamated in 1993 to become the maternity department of the new Leazes Wing of the RVI.

All hospital births in the city now took place on one site. The eminent obstetrician Professor Ranken Lyle would almost certainly have been delighted with this development.

The Bell's Court pioneers

Newcastle School of Medicine originated in 1832 when a small group of physicians and surgeons began giving lectures to medical apprentices in an auction room above the entrance to Bell's Court, a lane off Pilgrim Street.

Among the surgeons who lectured was John Fife, who was twice mayor of Newcastle and who received a knighthood in 1840. Fife's consulting rooms were in the Bell's Court building where the lectures were held. From 1837 to 1867 he was an honorary surgeon to the old Infirmary.

The other lecturers were surgeons Henry Glassford Potter, Alexander Fraser and Duncan McAllum and physicians George Fife, brother of John, and Samuel Knott.

The initial number of students attracted by the course was eight or nine and they included John Snow, who was to help pioneer the use of chloroform as an anaesthetic. Dr Snow administered chloroform to Queen Victoria when she gave birth to Prince Leopold in 1853 and at the birth of Princess Beatrice in 1857.

Significantly, he was the first to advance the theory, which proved to be correct, that cholera was a water-borne disease caused by pollution from cesspools, drains and sewage and he wrote about ways of preventing this serious illness. Dr Snow placed great emphasis on the provision of clean water, free from pollution. His theory of cholera transmission through water was a milestone in the early development of bacteriology.

In 1854, Snow traced the source of a cholera outbreak in Soho, London, to polluted water from a pump in Broad Street, helping to establish the truth of his theory. He persuaded the authorities to have the handle of the pump removed.

His attention had almost certainly been drawn to the question of cholera while he worked as an apprentice to a Tyneside surgeon during an outbreak of the disease in 1832. There were 306 deaths in Newcastle from the illness during this particular epidemic.

Top: Dr John Snow, one of the first students at the Bell's Court lectures. He advanced the theory that cholera is transmitted through water. Middle: Pioneering obstetrician and gynaecologist, Robert Patten Ranken Lyle. Right: The Gardener's Cottage which served for a time as a home for the majority faction of the Medical School.

Left: A recent picture of the derelict Barber Surgeons' Hall near Rye Hill. It became the home of the minority faction after the dissolution of the first Medical School.
Right: The coat of arms and motto of the Medical School on the side of the Northumberland Road college building.

A second course of lectures on medicine, surgery, anatomy, physiology and related subjects was held at Bell's Court in 1833-34. By then, however, it was felt that larger premises were needed.

Accordingly, in the autumn of 1834 the burgeoning school moved to new accommodation in the Hall of the Barber Surgeons Company in the Manors area of the town. The hall, which had been vacated by the Barber Surgeons, was close to the Holy Jesus Hospital.

The year of the move is generally regarded as the official foundation of the school and the organisation became known as the Newcastle upon Tyne School of Medicine and Surgery. The newly-acquired premises were renamed the Surgeons' Hall. The facilities included a medical museum. At this time the number of students attending lectures rose to twenty-six.

The courses continued in the hall until expansion of the nearby railway led to demolition of the building. But the railway company offered to provide an alternative home. In 1851, work began on the construction of a new hall at the top of Victoria Street, off Westmorland Road, in the west end of the town.

A bitter dispute arose between the lecturers of the school. Clashes of personality and professional rivalry may have been among the factors behind the problem.

The ostensible reason for the dispute was competition between two candidates for the post of surgeon to a Newcastle district of the Poor Law Union. A lecturer aspiring to this position believed a fellow lecturer, who was one of the Poor Law Guardians, had unfairly passed him over in favour of the other candidate.

The dispute resulted in heated scenes and two factions emerged. Failure to reach agreement led to the dissolution of the school in the summer of 1851. An undignified tug-of-war over possession of the museum items followed.

The Medical College building in Northumberland Road, now part of Northumbria University. It was used from 1948 until 1977 as the Dental Hospital and School.

It was an odd and unsatisfactory situation. One group of lecturers, the majority, founded a new school and became the "College of Medicine." They moved into temporary accommodation in the Gardener's Cottage in the grounds of the now demolished Barber Surgeons' Hall in the Manors. An extension to the cottage was built to give further space.

The other faction, the minority, became the "College of Medicine and Practical Science" and moved into the new Barber Surgeons' Hall in Victoria Street, close to Rye Hill. It was dubbed by many the "Rye Hill College".

But the majority group forged close links with Durham University and in October, 1852, moved from the Gardener's Cottage to premises built in Orchard Street, close to the Central Station. These premises were in the grounds of Westmorland House, which stood where Neville Hall, home of the Mining Institute, was later erected. The school building was designed by John Dobson.

Significantly, the Orchard Street premises were not far from the Infirmary at the top of Forth Banks. Students did not have to go far for practical instruction at the hospital.

The college had also taken over Westmorland House as well as its grounds, but the use of this mansion as a residence for medical students was dropped after a short period.

By the end of 1852 the links between the Orchard Street school and Durham University had been formalised and the college was known as the Newcastle upon Tyne College of Medicine in Connection with the University of Durham.

In 1857, unity between the rival colleges was at last achieved when the minority joined the majority. The majority's links with the university had proved a persuasive factor in healing the rift. A key figure in bringing the two sides together was Newcastle Infirmary surgeon Thomas Greenhow, who had first suggested the idea of setting up a medical school in the town.

The year 1870 brought the unified college into an even closer relationship with the university and it became the University of Durham College of Medicine. Expansion of student numbers continued and in 1879 there were 130. This made it the largest medical school in England outside London.

Among the long-serving lecturers during this period was the surgeon George Yeoman Heath, who was considered a brilliant teacher by his students. Heath, president of the college from 1874 until his death in 1892, was an honorary surgeon to the old Infirmary. His career as a lecturer had begun in the 1840s and he eventually became the college's first professor of surgery.

Other distinguished lecturers included Dr Edward Charlton, who served as honorary physician to the Infirmary from 1853 to 1874 and president of the college from 1872 to 1874; William Christopher Arnison, who became professor of surgery in 1892 and was honorary surgeon to the Infirmary from 1867 to 1897; and Dr George Hare Phillipson, later Sir George, a physician to the Infirmary from 1868 to 1896, a professor of medicine from 1876 to 1918 and president of the college from 1892 to 1918.

Eminent surgeon James Rutherford Morison, who developed an antiseptic paste which he used to treat wounded soldiers during the First World War.

Also noted for his valuable contribution was Frederick Page, house surgeon to the Infirmary from 1870 to 1880 and honorary surgeon from 1880 to 1900. Page was professor of surgery from 1899 to 1910.

Another eminent surgeon and fine teacher, James Rutherford Morison, served at the Infirmary from 1888 and became professor of surgery in 1910. His clinical teaching and the standard of his surgical work received high praise. During the First World War, Rutherford Morison pioneered the use of an antiseptic and astringent paste for wounds, known as BIPP (bismuth iodoform paraffin paste), while working at the First Northumberland War Hospital (St Nicholas, Gosforth).

These luminaries of the school were augmented by Dr Thomas Oliver, later Sir Thomas, an expert on industrial diseases, who was professor of physiology. One of his specialities was lead poisoning – a major problem among the women workers in the lead factories of Tyneside. Sir Thomas Oliver became president of the medical school in 1926.

Others who lectured at various times included George Haliburton Hume, a surgeon to the Infirmary from 1869 to 1905 and whose history of the hospital is still the authoritative work on the subject. Hume was the father of Newcastle heart physician, Dr William E. Hume and grandfather of Cardinal Basil Hume.

The careers of all these leading men, who held posts at the Infirmary and the school, illustrate that the hospital had become a key training ground for Newcastle's medical students. From its opening in 1906, the RVI took over this vital role.

In October 1889, impressive, newly-built premises for the college were officially opened in the city's Northumberland Road, then known as Bath Road. The ceremony was performed by the Mayor of Newcastle. The foundation stone had been laid by Algernon, Sixth Duke of Northumberland, in November 1887. The Orchard Street school building, which had become too small for the increasing numbers of students, was acquired by the North Eastern Railway.

The Northumberland Road college was built of red brick in Elizabethan style. Among its features were an anatomical theatre, a lecture theatre, an impressive examination hall, two dissecting rooms and a medical museum. An extension known as the Heath Wing, was completed in 1906. It included laboratories, lecture theatres and a cafe.

Medical students outside the Queen Victoria Road college building of the school in the 1950s.

The entire building still exists today as part of Northumbria University and is known as the Sutherland Building. The examination hall contains decorative plasterwork featuring the names of leading professors and lecturers of the school. It may be regarded as a memorial to these dedicated physicians and surgeons who spent their lives saving others and relieving suffering and who imparted their knowledge and experience to countless students.

The exterior of the building carries the motto of the school in Latin: 'Scire usum medendi.' This can be translated as 'To know how to mend', or 'To know how to put things right.' An alternative translation is 'To know how to care.'

In 1891, Dr George Redmayne Murray, who was born in Newcastle, was appointed a lecturer in bacteriology and comparative anatomy at the college.

Two years later, Murray became Heath Professor of Comparative Pathology and in 1896 was appointed an honorary physician to the old Infirmary, later transferring to the RVI.

It was while working in the city that Dr Murray pioneered the successful treatment of myxoedema, a condition caused by an under-active thyroid gland. In 1891, he demonstrated that extract from a sheep's thyroid gland was highly effective in combating this disorder. It was an important medical breakthrough.

Our account of the hospitals makes clear that during much of the 19th century the medical profession was almost exclusively the domain of men. However, the first women graduated from Newcastle Medical School in 1898. In becoming doctors, they began a female momentum which still gathers pace in our own day.

By 1920, there were seventy female students at the school. However, the first woman professor was not appointed until 1986. She was Professor Pat Kendall-Taylor, who held the chair of endocrinology.

Progress has now accelerated. Today, the majority of students at the school are women. It is a remarkable turnaround and a reversal of the male ascendancy of Victorian times.

After the First World War, eminent physician Sir David Drummond, who became president of the school in 1918, unveiled a memorial to the fifty-three students and graduates who lost their lives in the conflict. It must have been a poignant moment for him. Sir David, who served as president until 1926, had lost one of his own sons in the war. This distinguished doctor and lecturer became professor of medicine in 1911.

The entrance to the Faculty of Medical Sciences, Framlington Place.

Meanwhile, expansion of college places continued and in 1934 the number of students exceeded 500. Extra space had been created by expansion into the former Dame Allan's School building on the other side of Northumberland Road.

The school moved again in 1938 when a large, new, red-brick building was completed in Queen Victoria Road, opposite the RVI and on the corner with St Thomas Street. It still stands, next to the buildings of Armstrong College.

A year earlier the medical school had joined with Armstrong College to form King's College, Durham. It was known as King's College Medical School, University of Durham.

The new premises in Queen Victoria Road were occupied by the end of 1938 and the official opening took place in February the following year, only months before the start of the Second World War. The opening ceremony was performed by King George VI and the new premises were given his name. The building's proximity to the RVI was clearly a major advantage.

The old college premises in Northumberland Road were eventually taken over by Newcastle Dental Hospital and School.

In 1963, the medical school became part of the newly formed Newcastle University. Its origins in the early 1830s made it the university's oldest department.

The King George VI Building in Queen Victoria Road was replaced and a new era began on November 6, 1984, when a large, state-of-the-art, school was opened by the Queen Mother on the western side of the RVI.

It features two large buildings linked by a bridge corridor to the Leazes Wing of the hospital. These buildings, which house the Faculty of Medical Sciences, are named after novelist Catherine Cookson and William Leech, who were major benefactors of the university. The impressive main entrance to the school is situated in Framlington Place, behind Claremont Road.

In 2005 a clinical research centre was opened in the Leazes Wing.

A Newcastle medical school fit for the 21st century had been created. Expansion of undergraduate places continued and during the first decade of this century the total number of students rose to around 1,700, with an annual intake of 350.

The original doorway that led to the room at Bell's Court where the school had begun its life in the 1830s was installed at the end of a corridor in the new school at Framlington Place, a reminder that great achievements can spring from small beginnings.

Links with Durham and Malaysia

In 1998, Newcastle Medical School re-established its partnership with Durham University. Medical students of Durham underwent their Phase I studies at the Queen's Campus, Stockton, at the same time as those at Newcastle. The students from both sites then joined together to enter Phase II, which has been managed by Newcastle and undertaken mainly at eighteen teaching hospitals and at numerous GP surgeries around the North. The first Stockton intake under the Newcastle-Durham link-up took place in 2001.

The links with Durham are continuing. From 2017-18 Durham students starting their MBBS (Bachelor of Medicine and Bachelor of Surgery) programme will begin their studies in Newcastle. From 2018-19, all Durham students will be based in Newcastle for years one and two of the MBBS.

Another important development was the opening of a branch of Newcastle Medical School in Johor, Malaysia. The scheme was launched in 2009 and the Malaysian campus officially opened in 2011.

St Nicholas Hospital

One of the first Newcastle hospitals for those suffering from mental illness was opened at the northern end of the Warden's Close, outside the western Town Walls, in 1767.

A subscription fund to build the hospital had been started two years earlier, supported by Newcastle Corporation. Known simply as the Lunatic Asylum, it was designed by William Newton.

Mackenzie describes the situation of the asylum, at the north end of Bath Lane, as "retired and quiet". By around 1820 conditions at the hospital were appalling. He tells us that the asylum became frequently extremely overcrowded and that little attention was paid to providing fresh air and to cleanliness.

Mackenzie states: "The chains, iron bars, and dungeon-like cells, presented to the unhappy inmates all the irritating and melancholy characteristics of a prison, and at the same time were highly injurious to their health and lives."

The "dark and cold" cells, which opened on to a courtyard, were "less comfortable than cow-houses".

However, Newcastle Corporation took over the running of the asylum in the 1820s after all the subscribers had died. The corporation was unhappy with the way the institution had been run.

In 1824, they appointed Dr Noel Thomas Smith to take charge and he greatly improved conditions for the patients. They were now provided with "airing yards" where they could take exercise and enjoy the fresh air. Each class of patients had access to a day-room, and a separate gallery, warmed by hot air from fires and stoves below.

Mackenzie adds: "All the rooms are kept remarkably clean; and even the paupers are accommodated with warm, clean, separate beds, two or four in one room."

When Dr Smith first took charge of the asylum he found "six miserable wretches" chained down in their cells. This humane physician liberated them and according to Mackenzie they lived on to enjoy the freedom of the large garden which adjoined the house.

The Lunatic Asylum was mainly for the poor, but for patients with mental illness whose families were well-off financially a home known as St Luke's was opened in the Spital Tongues area, behind the ground eventually occupied by Fenham Barracks, in 1766. It was later rebuilt, enlarged and renamed the Bellegrove Retreat.

By the 1820s, this privately-run asylum contained twenty-four living apartments and could accommodate eight or nine patients of each sex.

Those men and women who were recovering were allowed to walk in the gardens or in a field adjoining the house, and they were occasionally permitted to take accompanied walks on the Town Moor and Castle Leazes.

According to Mackenzie, in the 1820s most of the patients at the Bellegrove Retreat had a sitting-room and bedroom, which were comfortable and "even elegant". They were all "neatly furnished, papered and carpeted".

Noisy or unruly patients were accommodated in a dormitory separate from the main building and walked in a separate garden.

It seems that all the residents were well fed. Mackenzie declares that they had "a good dinner of fish, beef, mutton, veal, fowls with vegetables, puddings etc, and excellent malt liquor, wine and sometimes a little punch, as may be thought proper".

Shower baths, portable warm baths, access to books from the circulating libraries and "harmless games" were among the other facilities provided.

Newcastle Lunatic Asylum and the Bellegrove Retreat were both closed in the 1850s. The asylum was eventually demolished and the Bellegrove Retreat house became a private residence. It was renamed Whiteknights and survives to this day.

Following closure of the asylum, the mentally ill poor of Newcastle were sent to asylums in County Durham.

Major change came in 1869 when a large, purpose-built hospital was opened on the outskirts of the town. Named the Newcastle upon Tyne Borough Lunatic Asylum, it was erected on farmland at Coxlodge, Gosforth, a short distance to the north of Salters Road.

The hospital had an area of land adjoining it where vegetables, fruit and other crops could be grown and patients could enjoy walks. Some of the male patients helped with the tasks of maintaining the grounds and growing produce. Livestock was also kept on what was, in effect, a farm attached to an asylum. Later, the amount of land available was increased.

Initially built to accommodate 250 patients, the asylum was to face problems of overcrowding as the number of admissions rose. In 1885, Newcastle City Council purchased extra land adjoining the site in order to expand the accommodation. The expansion consisted of two new wings, known as the east and west pavilions, which opened in 1887.

Meanwhile, with Newcastle gaining city status in 1882, the institution's name had been changed to the Newcastle upon Tyne City Lunatic Asylum.

A further major addition to the hospital was completed in 1900, enabling it to accommodate more than 800 patients. This expansion included a large recreation hall complete with a stage for shows.

St Nicholas Hospital, Gosforth. Viewed from one of the towers. The hospital opened in 1869.

In 1915, during the First World War, the asylum was converted into a military hospital for soldiers wounded in the conflict. The civilian patients were evacuated to other asylums, mainly in the North East. Named the First Northumberland War Hospital, the military hospital was returned to civilian use as an asylum in 1921.

During the 20th century, many significant improvements took place in the care and treatment of those suffering from mental illness and mental disability and the asylum at Coxlodge shared in these important developments. With the advent of the National Health Service in 1948 it was renamed St Nicholas Hospital.

From the last decades of the 20th century onwards the number of patients at St Nicholas was reduced as the emphasis switched to delivering care based within the community.

Smaller homes were provided in various areas of the city with the aim of developing as much independence as possible for suitable patients, backed by appropriate care and support. Parts of the hospital grounds and buildings were sold off, with some areas being redeveloped for housing.

A quiet, compassionate revolution in care had occurred over many years and services were now a far cry from the primitive 18th century asylum in Bath Lane.

Hanover Square to RVI

A surgical ward at the Fleming Memorial Hospital for Sick Children in its early years.

The first children's hospital in Newcastle was opened by a group of doctors in a house in Hanover Square, near the Central Station, in 1863. The numbers treated soared from fifty in-patients during the first year to 150 in 1885. Overcrowding had become a serious problem.

Wealthy Newcastle solicitor John Fleming came to the rescue in 1886 by offering to provide a large, purpose-built new children's hospital as a memorial to his wife, Mary, and as a replacement for the Hanover Square house. It was decided that a site on the Moor Edge, near the Great North Road, would be suitable. Appropriately named the Fleming Memorial Hospital for Sick Children, it was opened in 1888 by Lord Armstrong of Cragside.

Armstrong also became a benefactor of the hospital. He paid for an out-patients' clinic in City Road as a memorial to his wife, Lady Margaret, who had died in 1893. The clinic opened in 1896 and was on the opposite side of the road to the Holy Jesus Hospital. It replaced the Hanover Square house, which had been retained for a time as an out-patients' unit.

Another children's unit was the Babies Hospital, which opened in West Parade, on the corner with Westmorland Road, in 1925 and later moved to three large, adjoining houses in Leazes Terrace, close to the present day St James' Park football stadium.

Its origins could be traced back to 1917 when a nursery had been set up by Greta Rowell in West Parade for children whose mothers were working in the wartime munitions factories in the West End of the city.

During the Second World War. the Babies Hospital was evacuated to Blagdon Hall because of the air raid threat and it received strong support from Lady Ursula Ridley, wife of the Third Viscount Ridley of Blagdon.

The unit reopened at Leazes Terrace in 1948 and by this time it had been integrated with the RVI. The Babies' Hospital provided treatment with the then unusual feature of allowing mothers to stay at the hospital with their babies or young children while their offspring underwent in-patient treatment and recovery.

Eminent RVI and Newcastle General Hospital paediatrician Dr James Spence, later Sir James, was the leading advocate of this policy and today it is the norm for parents to stay with their youngsters in hospital. In 1942 he became the first professor of child health at Newcastle and also the first in the UK.

Sir James served the West Parade Nursery, the Babies Hospital, the RVI and

Newcastle General Hospital with distinction during a career in which he pioneered the speciality of paediatrics and was renowned worldwide for his work. He drew attention to the social aspects of ill health among children, citing poverty and deprivation as major factors.

At the RVI, Sir James developed a dedicated children's department and an out-patients' clinic in the former hospital governor's house. He was chief physician to the children's wards.

Sir James and a leading colleague, Dr Fred Miller, began the Newcastle One Thousand Families Study, which aimed to follow the first year in the lives of babies born in May and June 1947 in the city and which developed into a long-term project, still in progress and which followed those 'babies' into adulthood.

Born at Amble, Northumberland, Sir James Spence died in 1954. This outstanding physician had played a major role in the development of paediatrics.

From the 1960s onwards, the Babies Hospital provided surgery and was particularly noted for its work with the newborn. Eventually, however, these operations were moved to the Fleming.

After its foundation in Victorian times, the Fleming went on to provide the children of Tyneside and the surrounding area with much-valued service and became known for its family-friendly atmosphere.

Among later developments at the Fleming were a cleft palate and lip surgery service, a burns treatment unit and a neonatal surgery service. Accommodation for mothers to stay with their babies was provided from 1977 and later fathers and siblings were included.

The Fleming closed in 1987 and its services were transferred to the RVI. It had been a much-valued asset to the city. Today, the Great North Children's Hospital at the RVI is a major centre for the delivery of health care and treatment to the young.

The workhouse transformed

Newcastle General Hospital originated in Victorian times as an infirmary attached to a workhouse for the poor and evolved over the years into an important modern hospital providing key health services for the people of the city and beyond.

The workhouse was opened in 1840 by the Newcastle Poor Law Board of Guardians on land on the northern side of Westgate Road at the top of Westgate hill.

As well as the able-bodied poor, accommodation included provision for those suffering from illness or disability and for expectant mothers.

Pressure of numbers eventually led to the proposal that a hospital should be built on land close to the workhouse. Construction began in 1868 and it was officially opened on December 7, 1870, by Thomas Ridley, chairman of the Board of Guardians.

This first stone building surrounded three sides of a lawn area that faced on to Westgate Road. The lawn was divided by a wall that separated male and female patients. There were eleven wards.

The hospital continued to develop and grow throughout much of the late 19th century and into the 20th century. The number and variety of services offered increased enormously.

A ward block at Newcastle General Hospital.

The First World War brought a significant change. The workhouse buildings and a section of the hospital were taken over by the Army and used for the treatment of soldiers suffering from venereal diseases. At one point around 800 beds at the General were reserved for soldiers with sexually transmitted infections.

An important three-storey building – known as the New Infirmary Block - containing five wards had been opened in 1914. This initially catered for medical, child and TB patients. However, two new operating theatres were completed in 1926 and from then on surgical patients were accommodated in four of the wards.

In 1921, the name of the institution was changed to the Wingrove Hospital, the title Workhouse being dropped to indicate that patients were now drawn from the general population. The Board of Guardians also set up a separate administration to run the hospital.

Other developments included the provision of a large, purpose-built nurses' home with around 180 bedrooms, which was opened on the opposite side of Westgate Road in 1928. The home was linked to the hospital by a pedestrian tunnel running beneath the road.

In 1930, administration and control was handed over to Newcastle City Council's Health Committee and the hospital was renamed Newcastle General Hospital (NGH).

Under the Health Committee, the 1930s witnessed the NGH open a series of important additional facilities, including a cardiovascular department, a new children's department, a diabetic clinic, a thoracic surgery department, a new maternity unit, a new X-ray unit, a prostatic surgery department and a venereal diseases clinic.

In 1936, the hospital was given the use of Whitton Tower, Rothbury, as a convalescent home for children over five years of age. The benefactor was Sir Angus Watson and the home was named in memory of his wife. Younger children were accommodated at Wellburn House convalescent home in Ovingham.

By the late 1960s, the facilities at the General also included an accident and emergency department with two operating theatres, linked closely to the X-ray department, the Regional Neurological Centre, the Regional Radiotherapy Centre and Medical Physics Unit, departments for urology, surgery, and plastic surgery, a burns treatment unit and ante-natal and eye outpatients' clinics.

The urology department, which evolved from the prostatic surgery unit, performed Newcastle's first kidney transplant in 1964.

The administration block at Newcastle General Hospital, Westgate Road.

Today, most of the facilities which were provided at the NGH have been moved to the Freeman Hospital in High Heaton and the newly rebuilt RVI, but the site in Westgate Road still retains a few services such as the Centre for Ageing and Vitality and a minor injuries unit.

The NGH had developed from a workhouse hospital into a key component of Newcastle's health care services.

The Eye Infirmary

The Newcastle Infirmary for Diseases of the Eye was founded by the surgeons John Fife, later Sir John, and Thomas Greenhow in 1822. Its first home was a house in Brunswick Place. However, the demand for the services of the institution was so great that in 1824 it moved to a larger home in Prudhoe Street.

The poor suffering from various eye conditions were admitted as patients without any need for recommendation letters. Between 1822 and 1826 more than 3,000 were treated at this specialist infirmary.

Mackenzie, whose history of Newcastle was published in 1827, tells of 18 patients who were operated on for cataracts during the year ending March 1826, and asserts that these operations were a 'complete success'.

In 1885, came another change of location. The hospital moved to a newly built home in St Mary's Place. There were four wards and thirty-eight beds, plus an outpatients' department.

It was to remain at St Mary's Place until its closure in 1957. The land on which it stood was required for the development of the new Civic Centre and the hospital building proved too small for the increasing demands upon it.

Upon closure, patients were transferred to Walkergate Hospital in the East End of the city and an eye outpatients' clinic was opened at Newcastle General Hospital. For a time, child patients were treated at Walker Park Hospital, although later they too were admitted to Walkergate. Today, Newcastle's eye treatment services are based in the Claremont Wing of the RVI.

Fighting against TB

TB patients were treated at several locations in Newcastle at various periods, including the General, Fleming and Walkergate hospitals and the Northern Counties Chest Hospital. In addition, a chest clinic, also known as the TB Hospital, was opened in New Bridge Street in 1913. Newcastle Corporation funded the setting up of this unit, which was based at numbers 1 and 2 Ridley Villas.

The huge advance in the treatment of TB with the advent of streptomycin and later other antibiotics and the introduction of immunisation led to a decline in the number of patients attending the New Bridge Street clinic during the 1960s. It closed in 1972 after being used for a time to deliver other medical services.

The Northern Counties Chest Hospital was founded in 1878 and its first home was in Blackett Street. Patients were treated after being recommended by subscribers. In 1924, the hospital moved to premises in Westgate Road, but in 1930 came another move, this time to a large house, Derwent View, in Beechgrove Road, between Elswick and Westmorland roads in the West End of the city.

Closure came in 1978 and patients were transferred to the NGH chest unit, which had been reduced in size from two wards to one.

Ear, Nose and Throat Hospital

Newcastle Ear, Nose and Throat Hospital began life in 1877 in Clayton Street. It was set up by Dr Richard Ellis.

The familiar story of increasing demand resulted in a move to new premises on Rye Hill in the West End of the city in 1906. Later, the need for more space led to the acquisition of an adjoining property. The unit was also known as the Rye Hill Hospital. Its services were transferred to Newcastle General Hospital in 1962. Later, a renal dialysis unit was opened at Rye Hill.

Hunter's Moor

Hunter's Moor Hospital at Spital Tongues originated as the Home for Incurables, which was opened in 1884 by the St Mary Magdalene and Holy Jesus charity.

The Home for Incurables occupied a house known as Moor Lodge on the edge of Hunter's Moor. However, in 1893 a large, purpose-built home for the institution was opened in the grounds of the lodge and this was extended to accommodate child patients in 1911. During the 1930s the name of the centre was changed to the St Mary Magdalene Home. Moor Lodge was demolished.

After the advent of the NHS in 1948, the institution was renamed the Hunter's Moor Hospital and it became the Regional Neurological Rehabilitation Centre. 2007 saw the unit move to Walkergate Hospital.

The main Hunter's Moor buildings were demolished and Dame Allan's School redeveloped the site for its junior and infant sections.

The St Mary Magdalene and Holy Jesus charity today provides bungalows for older people at another site at Spital Tongues.

Sanderson Hospital

The Sanderson Hospital, Gosforth.

The Sanderson Hospital and School for disabled children could trace its origins to a home set up in a house at Whickham in 1888. It was then known as the W.J. Sanderson Home for Crippled Children and its aims were to 'clothe, feed and shelter crippled children from the Northern Counties', who were described as 'destitute', and to provide them with education, training in various trades and medical treatment.

Eleven years later the institution moved to Red House, at The Green, Wallsend. However, a continued rise in the number of children led to another move. This came in 1897 when a large, new building was opened in Salters Road, Gosforth, Newcastle, to accommodate both the home and school. A small hospital facility was incorporated within the building. The project had been made possible by charitable donations.

The foundation stone was laid in June 1896 by the wife of W.J. Sanderson, who was a Lord Mayor of Newcastle, an alderman of the city and a JP. Alderman Sanderson had been a prime mover in setting up the home and helping to fund it.

The site at Gosforth featured a large garden and the school rooms were provided with an open-air verandah on which the youngsters could be taught during the summer and on which they could rest.

As well as a basic education, the children were given instruction in a number of skills aimed at helping them in later life. Boys were taught shoemaking, tailoring and gardening and girls received instruction in cookery, dressmaking and other domestic work.

During the 1920s, advanced orthopaedic treatment services were developed at the site under eminent surgeon James Rutherford Morison.

A new hospital opened at the home in 1924 and later the name of the institution was officially changed to the W.J. Sanderson Orthopaedic Hospital School for Children. Many of the youngsters were suffering from paralysis of limbs and the effects of TB and rickets.

Over the decades following the introduction of a surgery service there was a major decline in the number of children required to stay at the hospital and school on a long-term basis. Modern operations enabled the youngsters to be discharged to their homes and to attend ordinary schools after only a short stay.

This decline in long-term child patients freed space for the introduction of adult orthopaedic treatment at the hospital and the development of a physiotherapy service. These services eventually moved to the Freeman Hospital. The Sanderson buildings have now been demolished.

The shipbuilder's gift

The Walker Accident Hospital, which was used to treat injured shipyard workers in its early years.

In 1870, the Walker Accident Hospital was opened to treat workers injured in shipyard and factory accidents. Shipbuilder Charles Mitchell, of the Low Walker Yard, paid for the hospital to be built.

This new medical facility, in Airey Terrace, Walker, in the East End of the city, was opened in May 1870 by the Mayor of Newcastle, James Morrison, in the presence of members of the council and the local board of health.

Charles Mitchell was also present and he told the gathering that it was proposed that each workman in Walker contribute a penny ha'penny per week towards the maintenance of the hospital.

Originally, the hospital had sixteen beds, which could be increased to twenty in an emergency.

The first patient was Patrick Butler, who had suffered a fractured leg when he fell from staging (scaffolding) placed against the side of a ship in one of the yards.

A change of role came in 1960 when under the NHS much of the unit was converted to treat gynaecology patients and a new operating theatre was opened. By this time it was known as Walker Park Hospital. The gynaecology unit closed in 1977.

Dentistry at Handyside Arcade

Newcastle Dental Hospital and School was founded in 1895 in Nelson Street in the city centre. By the early 1900s, it had become clear that larger accommodation was needed and in 1906 the hospital moved from Nelson Street to premises in the Handyside Arcade, Percy Street.

The arcade was an unusual location for a dental hospital and school, being next to a billiard room and a boot repair factory.

This somewhat out-of-the-ordinary accommodation certainly did not prevent the institution from gaining increased recognition - in 1910, Durham University introduced a Licentiate in Dental Surgery and during the 1920s added Bachelor and Master degrees.

Integration with the medical school came during the next decade when the dental hospital and school moved from the Handyside Arcade to premises in the grounds of the RVI. Buildings that had been part of the former Ministry of

The former Dental Hospital and School in Queen Victoria Road, which opened in 1932.

Pensions Hospital were taken over and a new, purpose-built home was added to these, fronting on to Queen Victoria Road.

Shipping businessman Sir Arthur Munro Sutherland gave £12,600 towards the cost of the buildings and equipment. The new home of the dental hospital and school was officially opened in early 1932.

The school was renamed the Sutherland Dental School in recognition of the generosity of Sir Arthur. In 1937, it became an official department of the Medical School of King's College, Durham University.

However, a steady increase in the numbers of patients and students led to a rethink in the 1940s. The decision was taken to seek larger, alternative accommodation. In 1948, the institution moved to the former home of the medical school in Northumberland Road.

Aneurin Bevan, Minister of Health and founder of the NHS, opened the Northumberland Road dental hospital and school in 1948. Sir Arthur Munro Sutherland had again stepped in to help the institution, this time contributing £50,000 towards equipment.

During the early 1970s work began on building a fifth dental hospital and school on the western side of the RVI site in Richardson Road. It was officially opened by the Duke of Northumberland on May 29, 1978. This state-of-the-art hospital is next to the medical school and RVI.

The former home of the dental school in Northumberland Road is now part of Northumbria University and has been renamed the Sutherland Building. The site of the Handyside Arcade is today occupied by the Eldon Garden shopping precinct.

The pioneering Freeman

The Freeman Hospital opened its doors to patients in 1977 and was officially opened the next year by Prince Charles. Situated in Freeman Road, High Heaton, it was initially equipped with more than 800 beds and cost £15m to construct.

The Freeman delivers a wide range of services to patients from the North East region and has been a pioneer in transplant surgery.

In 1987, Britain's first successful heart transplant to save a child was performed at the hospital, and from 2003 it has offered a service which provides 'mechanical hearts' while patients await transplant operations.

Surgeons at the Freeman also perform lung transplants. They blazed a trail when they carried out the first single and double lung transplants in Europe.

In addition, the hospital is an important regional urology centre, that provides treatment for conditions including prostate and kidney problems. Services are also available to treat patients with liver and pancreatic disorders.

In 2009, the Freeman opened the Northern Centre for Cancer Care which provides state-of-the-art services to patients. It is the largest such centre in the North of England and features the latest, advanced radiotherapy equipment.

The centre works in close co-operation with the Sir Bobby Robson Cancer Research Unit, which is located at the Freeman, to carry out programmes of clinical trials.

Green oasis – the conservatory at the RVI. It linked the nurses' home to the main hospital building.

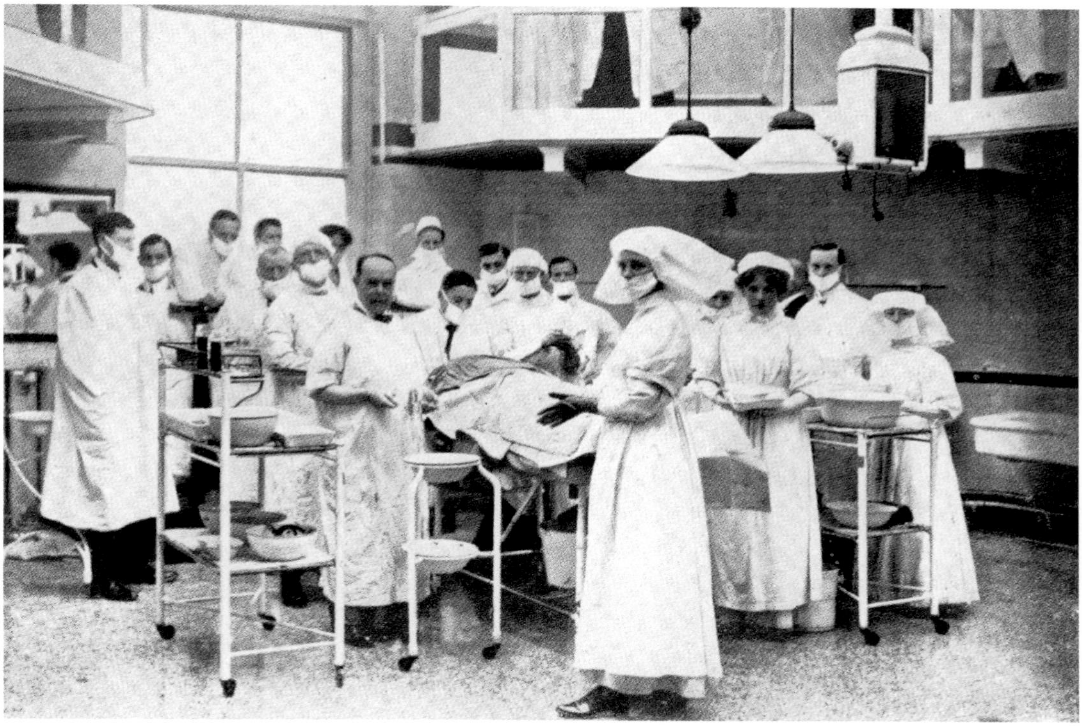

Top: Emeritus Professor Fred Page, foreground next to trolley, operating at the RVI in 1911 as the guest of Professor Rutherford Morison.
Above: A selection of Newcastle nurses' badges.

Dr Ethel Williams

The Northern Women's Hospital in Osborne Road, Jesmond, was set up by Dr Ethel Williams in 1917. Dr Williams, an active campaigner for women's suffrage, came to Newcastle in the 1890s and in 1906 was the first woman to become a medical General Practioner in the city. She is also said to have been the first woman to regularly drive a car in Newcastle. The location of the Northern Women's Hospital is now the site of the Nuffield Health Newcastle private hospital.

Dr Ethel Williams.

Postscript

Surveying the last 200 years, it can be seen that Newcastle has been and continues to be a medical centre of great significance, both in terms of delivering health services to the people of the North East and as one of the UK's most important training grounds for the physicians and surgeons of the future.

Those vital roles continue at the RVI, the Freeman Hospital, many other hospitals in the North and the medical school of Newcastle University. Let us conclude by declaring our highest regard for these humane endeavours, past and present.

Below: An early view of the RVI from a postcard.
Bottom: Resident nursing and medical staff of the RVI, 1916.

Principal sources consulted and further reading

The History of the Newcastle Infirmary. George Haliburton Hume (Andrew Reid, Newcastle, 1906).

A History of St Nicholas Hospital, Newcastle-upon-Tyne, England, 1869-2001. Logan Ewing (AuthorHouse, 2009).

The Newcastle upon Tyne School of Medicine, 1834-1934. G. Grey Turner and W.D. Arnison (Andrew Reid, Newcastle, 1934).

The Infirmary, Newcastle upon Tyne, 1751-1951. W.E. Hume (Andrew Reid, Newcastle, 1951).

Childbirth in Newcastle upon Tyne (1760-1990). Derek Tacchi (Bewick Press, Whitley Bay, 1994).

Descriptive and Historical Account of the Town and County of Newcastle upon Tyne, including the Borough of Gateshead. E. Mackenzie (1827).

A History of Gateshead. Frank Manders (Gateshead Corporation, 1973).

The Medical School of Newcastle upon Tyne. Dennis Embleton (1890).

NGH 1870-1966, The History of Newcastle General Hospital. George Hurrell and George P. Harlan (Newcastle upon Tyne Hospital Management Committee, printed by Hindson and Andrew Reid, Newcastle, 1966).

The Fleming Memorial Hospital for Sick Children, Newcastle upon Tyne. G. Dale, J. Donald and J. Wagget.

Hospitals. Lynn Redhead (Newcastle Libraries and Information Service, 1996).

Bygone Spital Tongues. Olive Taylor. (Newcastle Libraries and Information Service, 1993).

100 Years of the RVI, 1906-2006. Edited by John Walton and Miles Irving, various authors (Newcastle upon Tyne Hospitals NHS Trust, 2006).

Medicine in Northumbria. Essays by various authors (The Pybus Society for the History and Bibliography of Medicine, 1993).

Newcastle School of Medicine 1834-1984. Sesquicentennial Scrapbook. Compiled by Gordon Dale and F.J.W. Miller (The Faculty of Medicine, University of Newcastle upon Tyne, 1984).

Peacock Hall at Newcastle's RVI.